Under Shadows of Stars

Under Shadows of Stars

Poems by

Annie Bien

Kelsay Books

© 2017 Annie Bien. All rights reserved. This material may not be reproduced in any form, published, reprinted, recorded, performed, broadcast, rewritten or redistributed without the explicit permission of Annie Bien. All such actions are strictly prohibited by law.

Cover photo by: NASA, ESA and the Hubble Heritage Team (STScI/AURA)-ESA/Hubble Collaboration

ISBN: 13-978-1-947465-20-6

Kelsay Books
Aldrich Press
www.kelsaybooks.com

*To my mother and father, to my teachers,
His Holiness the Fourteenth Dalai Lama,
Khyongla Rato Rinpoche,
and my husband, Paul Merwin*

Acknowledgments

Autumn Sky: "Dance Scene 1989—NYC"
Shale: Extreme Fiction for Extreme Conditions: "Intervals in Moonglow"
Mockingheart Review: "The Third Eye"

Contents

Behind the Scrim	13
The Third Eye	15
An Interval with a Small Yet Seemingly Great Moment	16
Tumbleweed	17
Kodiak Bear	19
From JFK to West 72nd Street	21
Dance Scene 1989—NYC	23
The North Tower North Tower	25
Perigee	27
Columbus Park, Manhattan Chinatown	28
The Belasco Theatre	29
Sleepless Mother	30
Intervals in Moonglow	31
Beauty as a Metaphor for Being a Good Person	34
Floating Dust	35
An Interval with a Medium Moment	36
Midsummer Spring	37
The Waterfall	41
Reading Before the Lines	42
Fare Well	43

About the Author

༈ ཇི་ལྟར་བུ་མོ་གཞོན་ནུའི་རྨི་ལམ་ན།
བུ་ཕོ་བྱུང་ཞིང་ཤི་བ་དེས་མཐོང་ནས།
བྱུང་ནས་དགའ་ཞིང་ཤི་ནས་མི་དགའ་ལྟར།
ཆོས་རྣམས་ཐམས་ཅད་དེ་བཞིན་ཤེས་པར་གྱིས།

*Just as in the dream of a young girl when she came
upon a boy then saw him die— she was joyous
at having met and unhappy at his death:
know all phenomena as like this.*
      —Samadhiraja Sutra, Chapter 9, 43a

Behind the Scrim

Just as in the dream of a young girl

The old Victorian appeared, dilapidated;
staircases encircled both sides of the foyer.
The smell of wood souring
as rooms branched off landings, bookcases
crammed with leaning tomes, ornate lamps
warmed the way by incandescent lights.

A door ajar invited her to the inner sanctum.
Inside, the Art Deco rooms of her parents glimmered.
She leapt across creaking beams, alighting into a room
of floor-to-ceiling glass. Outside, clouds billowed across the
skyline
of a Woolworth Building skyscraper

where she came upon a boy then saw him die—

He sat in a velvet chair. They knew each other. From forever
ago, but this was their first meeting in this lifetime. His fingers
reached for her—

she was joyous at having met and

—his legs stretched, his cheekbones disappeared in the mist.
She could hear him sing, feel his hand slip away—and she wept—
not yet, not yet—

unhappy at his death:

She suddenly remembered. Here in this room, they were

once very old together.
                        He whispered in her ear, a vow from before.
                                Then, the cat nuzzled her awake:

know all phenomena as like this.

The Third Eye

The swan, wings spread wide,
lowers feet first toward the pond,
feathers pearling water:
between alighting
and lifting, the sun casts
a swan shadow,
an imprint of wings
and dappled water
of an illusory moment
vanishing
into reverie.

An Interval with a Small Yet Seemingly Great Moment

Last night in my near-waking dream,
a warehouse of many-ceilinged windows
spread opaque light upon iron railings.
Staircases disappeared into brightness. I held
a rainbow packet of crayons. My cat

jumped from my arms, up the staircase
into your lap. The crayons
spilled, melting colors.
Your fingers fanned. Light rays.
My cat stared. You told me:
I will hold him.

On the first-floor landing, a glass case
enclosed a radio, projecting my teacher young
—a visual film clip floats from his sentences—
He walks alone on the plateau. Melting.
Yellow flowers yield to yaks, grass folds under
their rhythmic steps, jangling bells from their braided hair.

My teacher laughs, a soundless wheeze. His sister
holds a telephone in her hand. She stares
into perforated holes: she hears him call
her name. He stands in the phone
in her mind, small, fixed:

Such is life, our meeting and parting.

The crayons melt into variegated light.
You read the letter I wrote. I know you will
leave. You fold the paper. Soundless.
Though I don't hear you: your echo resounds.

Tumbleweed

In the wind: Shhhhh—hhhhhhhhh—

Balls of dried plants roll
across the road—in catch and release—
where matted locks of dead branches
tumble across speaking runes of desert sand.

Daddy drives the OK Chevy sedan—
all ninety-nine dollars of it—
on Highway 99:

My head leans across my brother's lap,
puppylike, lolling toward the window,
a dried sour plum pressed on my tongue
to keep from throwing up.

Tumbleweed, as though driven with life and breath,
trips across the mirage of lifelessness
under short-shadowed sun. Spines of dried hulls
settle in our front yard after the sandstorm.

You are a lucky four-year old, Daddy said.
I had not yet met the child whose face
hardened at the sight of me and demanded:

What's the matter with your eyes? Jap Zero!
Dahdahdah dah dow—pshoo
His imaginary machine gun shot at me
—over and over—his freckled face streaked in glee.

Those were innocent days when Daddy declared:
We are so happy! One big happy family!

Mommy clenched her jaw so hard her chin
wrinkled like a dried prune. She closed her eyes.
Later she told me who she saw over and over—a woman.
Soldiers dragged her away. She never described
the troughs of afterbodies. But I know
she saw them. Later she said: *I was lucky I wasn't pretty.*
We named you, An, after Peace.

The tumbleweed skipped across the desert. A hiss of wind.

Kodiak Bear

The gutters rattled with rainwater
as my father's compasses etched arcs
of exactitude. Parametric equations
detailed by his mechanical pencil,
the slide rule, ruling and unruling
his universe. The abacus clicked,
his mathematical prayer beads.
I can't tell you more. It's classified
he said, *but not like want ads.*

He modeled the parka, turning around;
the pelt of an unfortunate wolf rimmed the hood,
a poor being stereotyped by Red Riding Hood,
a voiceless lone howl pulled over his head.

Daddy's lungs, pockmarked,
scarred from rheumatic fever,
diptheria, typhoid, cigarettes
without filter since everybody smoked
during the War to think or not think—
day by day the unseen pink wore down

more ragged, like old sponges on the kitchen sink,
rimmed with grease. When he exhaled
his chest shuddered north-south-east-west
accompanied by an accordion wheeze.

He swallowed tepid tea:
The boss stole my work, he showed it as his own,
no raise, they thought he was brilliant—I am—
My mother put her finger on his lips.
Stop. There are bills to pay.

A young girl listened to them whisper,
drawing mournful princes and princesses
wandering in Beardsley forests of India ink,
wondering what life would be like if dreams
were waking time and waking time dreams.
Someday I will turn the page after the fairy tale ends.

From JFK to West 72nd Street

1969. The first visit to New York City.
The long black polka-dot dress: a contrast-dot empire waist
with white ruffles, an artificial rose. My fancy dress.

The tourist antennae tune into the frequency:
A long dress at a matinee? Observe.
Next time, my dear, research.

In 1981 a casting director would ask: *Have you ever been
on Broadway?*
"I've walked on it." The panel chuckles.
So I'm not immediately chucked out.

Now the waiters at O'Neal's, all bowtied,
ooze handsomeness. Aunt Nina takes us to the New York
City Ballet. *Swan Lake*. Tschaikovsky. Tutus and feathers.

The dancers are more than a coffee table book could
ever reveal. Curtain calls. Then the 66th Street subway.
Aunt Nina says: *You need to do this once. Here's a nickel token.*

Parental fear envelops me. Then she sprints by—a ballerina—
grey floral chiffon, high heels, translucent skin, netted chignon,
makeup still intact. I want to sprint too. In high heels.
The IRT 1 train screeches in. But we wait. Life races by.

1977. Mattresses: stained, partly burnt, upended against a chain-
link fence. Car skeletons. Litter streaks on grass patches along
the Van Wyck Expressway.

I remember Aunt Nina: *Once the traffic was so bad I peed in my
patent leather purse. Threw it onto the side of the road. Handbags
on the Grand Central! In America, even the moths are clean.*

Handbags appear. The cab driver rolls the window down, tosses a gum wrapper. Exhaust mixes with summer sweat and heat. We have missed the Blackout. No unlit skyscrapers. Instead we will sit in a darkened audience awaiting lights.

My stomach flutters with pipe dreams: Alvin Ailey, Martha Graham, Merce Cunningham. We arrive at West 72nd Street.

Dance Scene 1989—NYC

Take the F train to Manhattan to Twenty-third Street,
walk to Nineteenth Street between Fifth Avenue

and Avenue of the Americas—the map of North
South and Central Americas in the faces

of the dancers squeezing into the elevator, bubbles
of laughter, to the eleventh floor: Alina from Cuba,

Beatriz from Puerto Rico, Julio from Argentina,
Robert from Texas, Kevin from Massachusetts,

the motley modern dance ladies with unshaved
armpits, Mother Gaia thighs next to the sylphs

in pink silk-ribboned toe shoes, grey plastic pants
to take off more sweat on already evaporated frames.

Ernie tells me—The word is don't pick up the lettuce girl
too quickly or she'll fart, and then you have to carry

her all across the stage with your head hid under her
skirt. He winks. Then Ernie, Jack, Harry, Greg don't come

to class anymore; I visit them in hospitals look at
their wan smiles, faces pale then dot with lesions.

At 159th Street in the Harkness
Pavilion, suitable for ballet dancers, I sit with John

wearing a New York City Ballet cap. He takes off
the cap and shows me the X and O circles on his head

marked for radiation. He holds my hand and weeps
—no tears—they've all dried now, Annie.

I remember him in class, long legs start at my waist,
in black tights and white t-shirt, Giacometti-slim

but elastic like a rubber band. He always says hello,
calls my name like I'm his best friend in the world.

My mother—he says—*won't visit me, she doesn't believe
in my illness. Sit with me, please.*

We sit together. He dies alone.
I still see him, making semaphores with his legs, mid-leap.

The North Tower North Tower

The skyline shifts. The North Tower spews a slate chrysanthemum, a once-solid unshakable-looking edifice collapses, collapses inward. Confetti-like metal catches sunlight, spewing debris: ash mixed with heat, swallowed into city streets, unrolls toward the East River, the Statue of Liberty, into the bay. The tower collapses in a groan. Slow then too quick. Smoke unrolls like waves curling toward a shore. It is not the moon tide but burn tide, tiny scraps of life hitting our faces.

The Trade Towers that we could see from our window to prove we weren't far from Manhattan, that it was okay to move to Brooklyn . . .

The skyline. The North Tower spews. A slate chrysanthemum, unshakable edifice, inward. Confettilike metal. Debris, ash, heat, swallowed city, unrolling East River, the Statue of Liberty, the bay. The tower groans. Slow. Too quick. City streets, waves curl toward a shore. Tiny scraps of life hit our faces.

The North Tower. A slate chrysanthemum, inward. Confetti-like metal. Ash, heat, swallowed city. The tower groans.

The Tower. The groans. The collapse. The roll. The ash. The swallowed city. The groans.

I wake up. Night. We've been silent during daylight. New York City speechless. But for sighed whispers. Restaurants with diners, cutlery tapping. We cook and can't eat. We listen to the same footage on the barely visible television screen. Our antenna dissolved into the North Tower.

I rewatch the North Tower fall. My mind rewinds the postcard-perfect day. Our rooftop. The North Tower. The eleventh day of September. Chrysanthemum. Spew. Plume. Again. Again. The towers. Maybe after the smoke they will resurrect. They won't. I don't want to sleep. Don't want to dream. That. I doze.
The North Tower spews slate chrysanthemum.

The next day, my teacher's disciple, a kindly monk, says to me, "When you have that dream and wake up, try this. Inhale and exhale. Relax and count your breath. See if you can count very slowly. Start again if you see the towers. Inhale and exhale. Rest your mind."

Perigee

Wolf moon magnifies my mother's white hair,
dawn ghosts the winter skyline—the ashen orb

rises into night alongside her face:
she no longer searches for heaven,

earth, sky, no search for the exact time, for the location
of departure. I watch you, Mother: your eyes review

the years of reality under shut lids, halting breath,
your pulse— for now—a quivering hospital gown.

I hold your hands the way you once held mine,
fingers laced—raveling thread—

we wait, on both sides: you about to be released
from unknowing to known unknowing, and I

touch your fingers—time to let go—a second hand
circles around and around—*what's the time*

what's the time—labored—your voice, echoes
from a well—streaks upon the brain, dust pocketed

in synapses. Those words we exchange,
decried as outdated by poets—

but for me as child—*I'm so proud of you*—
a tonic. And for you—*I love you very much.*

Your entire body, hooked to oxygen, smiles.
You envelop me still—fading mother and daughter.

Columbus Park, Manhattan Chinatown

The mah-jong players sit at stone tables, their hands "wash tiles"—a distinctive clicking and rubbing sound evoking memories of my mother scrubbing laundry across the washboard—their faces knit in silent strategy, an occasional utterance of *peng*, "touch." Pink petals swirl around the just-bloomed cherry tree, pollen affixing small granules of spring on my nose and eyes. Flower scents blend with duck fat and soy sauce, steamed buns stuffed with barbecued pork. Food—*fan*—rice, the mantra of a Chinese family—be it the slurp of noodles, the thermos of tea, burping or chattering full-mouthed. Along the sidewalk a man reads the fortunes of passersby, shifting the tin of oracular wood sticks. Chinese opera singers rehearse near the bandshell.

Sporting the universal bubble-cut black permanent wave, a group of women lift their arms and step in unison tai-chi movement. The two-stringed *erhu* player draws his bow in woeful tune, accompanied by the percussive drub of basketball players shouting, shooting hoops: Italian, black, Chinese. This former slum known as Five Points still harbors generations of immigrants who come and go.

If we had moved into Manhattan Chinatown, I might have known Cantonese as well as Mandarin. I might be able to order dim sum in what used to be considered by the locals as "real" Chinese. Today many dialects float in the air. A woman walks by wafting mothballs from her wool coat: into my mind comes Mommy's garment bag of camphored cheongsams in Bakersfield, my feet plunging down her pumps playing grownup in her closet.

The Belasco Theatre

You appear with residual blue glitter on your eyelid and sweatpants, kinesiology tape pasted on diagonals across your neck, a wink sealed with a smile.

Last night's invitation, a maroon velvet seat—last row orchestra—the buzz of voices, our sing-along, the lights honed on your fragile yet explosive presence swarm into my mind. A memory sweep of refurbished Tiffany lamps and retouched murals, anticipation walking downstairs to the ladies' sign, a cameo bust profile. A rarity of many stalls for women, tiled floors soundboards for clicking heels, and asymmetrical clothing contrast the Neo-Georgian architecture recalling long full skirts and tight corsets, dark suits. For your show, the men's queue will take longer. The remodeling has removed some mustiness and properness, but not the energy exuding from backstage. When the house lights go dark and the stage brightens, generations of memories are born, now including yours, from transforming daytime client to new friendship imbued with magic.

Good poetry leaves a strong echo, the Sanskrit poets say *dhvani*. After all is done, you turn your head—and like an evocative perfume, recall the voices, feel the touch and retraction of a stranger's sleeve on a shared seat arm, shins pressing a seat back, hear and smell varied breaths, the warm bodies stepping across you.

We greet each other for your morning workout. You point to aches and pains. The echo of the theatre returns. Every time I think of it I will think of you. Your hand touches mine.

Sleepless Mother

Last night, toes up, horizontal,
I remembered Mommy,
right hand clutching a balled tissue:

I have a secret. I can't sleep. I can't—
share it.

She exhaled—half sigh—half moan—
the bougainvillea yawned forward
and the azalea tilted open-jawed toward us,
a curl of jasmine scent dropped tendrils—

Maybe we could encircle her darkness
with matchlit bright afternoon.

Chinese people hold secrets
till death, the chef's secret pork bun
ingredient will be lost. Daddy and I
had snake at our wedding—disgusting—
the War—but ours was a love match.

Later I dug through her diaries from 1947:

My mind wastes away.
What for, Aurora College for Women—
my memory—they will put me away—
I am memorizing dates and addresses.

The last days, the secret didn't matter.
Moved out of emergency, her mind a crystal,
her hearing sharp, she speaks:
Annie-ah. *Wo hao ai ni.*
(*I love you very much.*)
Always have, she says in English.

Intervals in Moonglow

I peel off moments into my diary:

Day/Night 1. Interval with the small things

I dreamt you led me between two walls, very narrow, my head wouldn't fit even if I sucked my stomach in—then you pulled my hand—

A door opens and shuts. I try to hide, then see it's you—Mommy—no longer dead from five years before. My right hand clasps yours—once mine fit into your palm:

> *Your breath barely grazed the pillow that last day, you only slept. I remembered the times you sang me to sleep. Your hand patted my arm to a distracted tune from your childhood as your eyes gazed upon the waves sweeping your memories into Repulse Bay. . . . When walking the hill overlooking the hospital, the moon swelled in magnificent relief, magnifying our temporary state. I didn't want to disturb you in the room; I wanted to be uplifted, just in case it was the last day—just in case it was not. Some tears fell, these are the it's-okay-to-go-don't-feel-burdened-by-us tears. I have heard from the lamas that you hear everything when death is near—voices may babble but all thoughts are sonorous. This is when verbs are infinite and you read all minds. . . .*

Then—sweat under the covers—blue illuminated 4:30 AM—a radio announcer dissolves our hand-clasped dream state. I awaken: my heart-pounding-into-dawn-consciousness is reluctant to leave your visitation. Good-bye.

Night/Day 2. Interval with the medium things

We have not yet met in this moment, though once my most-beloved from my future and a nonremembered enemy in my past, or perhaps once most-beloved-reluctantly lost in my past and unwilling-to-accept-as-enemy in the future.

Here you stand in front of me: one eye glistens blue and the other is flecked with gold sparks on a green sea. Some gust of wind blows a curl over your brow. Before I fell asleep, I thought fleetingly of the space between imagination and reality: the tip of your head. Turning away from the optical eye to the mind's eye, unjudged by conventional reality as real. You walk toward me, my friend from infinite rebirths.

This jungle vine mixed with camellias, the steam of the greenhouse and dirt on the garden floor, the art deco room in the middle of the Victorian house that opens onto a view of the Woolworth building—you reassure me, this is as real as being awake is fleeting. Sometimes when here, in this recurring dreamworld, I am alone, searching for the center of the mandala. But this time, you drape your coat around me. I am the unseen shadow; you are vivid, tall. From the window, we watch the clouds obscure and reveal cityscape, blown by a cool breeze. My arms hold your waist; your arms, a banyan tree, embrace me.

Such is your visitation, the main character who fell out of the sky into my notebook. Before so vague, now I hear your voice, a low amused murmur sharing a secret; the veins on the back of your right hand, your long fingers entwine mine.

Day/Night 3. Interval with a great thing

At the crown of your head, a small Buddha glows, radiant; his eyes hover over your third eye: the place between your brow vibrates. The light of sunrise on morning clouds, pink, iridescent, of no visible light source, pours down through the crown of your head. Golden nectar infuses your body. Radiant sparks catch sunlight from golden skin and the voice of your teacher melts into you, suffusing your mind with dawn sky. The moment vanishes, as you do into molecules, into atoms, into universe, and stars, acacia trees, sandalwood forests, the buds on the narcissus not ready to bloom, ice caps, the polar bear breathing a cloud of cold, the whale diving away from the debris left over the surface of the earth, the sloth clinging to a vine, upside down, a snake winding its way as the liana. Your mind settles upon a tiny glowing syllable, *HUM*, growing in brightness. The shape of the letter begins to erase itself from bottom to top—*OOH*, the sounds seems to say—*HAA*—a release of breath, *MMM*—eases into an echo radiating outward as the universe. The tiny Buddha mixes into flesh, blood, bones, his smile fans the body. You look up. It is the same room you have lived in for years, the cats running across the hardwood floor murmuring and squeaking—because one doesn't know how to meow, the other translates into purr and wow. Yet it is a totally new room, new dust alights in old places. Arising from an abandoned fixed view, the room is veiled by sameness. On this evening, the clouds obscure the sun and ebbing daylight announces the everyday pond of fish swimming among reeds—flicking tales of infinite lives. I hear my fingers tap, my witnesses to fragile remembrance.

Beauty as a Metaphor for Being a Good Person

Gingko leaves deepen
as summer swarms into Brooklyn—
an Aeolian breath lifts
moisture off the forehead,
one season exits in forgetful fits:
a rainstorm, a burst of sun,
wind, spring pollen awhirl
tamped down, nature speckling
a city street, the afternoon damp
alights on my upper lip.

Wherever I am, I carry
the echo of your voice,
notes on a staff
playing a tune,
even if you forget:
the words we have shared
fall into
spaces
between phrases,
the way a conversation can breathe
the ending of each other's thoughts.
When I close my eyes,
when I blink,
when I turn,
no one sees
what I see.
Your smile.

Floating Dust

Nautical nods: ocean sprays
waves of floating dust upon rocks.
A tip of land anchors
my body in countable moments
against the drift of definite speed.

My mind, a-jumble, imagines
your shoulders turning, your eyes
reveal a sea of blues.

The pace toward shore, deliberate,
inevitable as the earth turns
away seasickness, a zephyr suggests:
some never see this Earth, her scars cut
not by herself but by those who only
see themselves, deep gullies not of longing.

Embrace of the earth underfoot,
even as I follow the shadows
of women I have never met:

the generations who followed
three steps behind, with bowed heads,
with Confucian values, swept dull in confusion,
numbed by grievous husbands—jealous women—
dulled women, carrying groceries, burdens with bowed
backs, waiting and longing for the story to change,
muted in the silence tied to an imaginary world of expectation,
of a promise of insubstantial deliverance:

Look here. There's a mist where every dewdrop
carries the image of your face evaporating
into the sky. And I, alone, can always carry
the image of you in secret.

An Interval with a Medium Moment

In the third watch between dreaming and waking,
a meeting—illusionlike dream-reality billows
toward illusionlike early morning:

It is still timeless evening when she is neither
herself nor other, looking at her arm that is not her arm.

He sits next to her, the blackness of his tuxedo a blue sheen,
his white shirt an uplight upon his face.

Something amiss under the candelabra reveals shaving lather
obscuring the curve of his right jaw.

Her hand squeeze reaches his eyes. She looks at his face
seemingly neutral, until she senses the smile envelop her hand.

Her mind pitches forward into space—their minds meet—
traverse consciousnesses. She awakens to pre-morning,
her heart apace. The clock moves a minute
forward, the streetlight from last night still on:

I say hello to you, good morning. In previous lives
we knew each other well, held hands
not in dreams but in daylight.

What this day will bring, a sound resonates—
though seemingly alone, not alone, for infinite lives
not alone—but solitary.

Midsummer Spring

All winter, plywood boards covered the thought
of trees and lawn, of time leaping forward.
Blossoms of spring dropped into midsummer,
the heat hewed pressed linen into limpness.
Then one Saturday, a field of grass and a fence,
people walking through a gate toward slim trees,
limbs in fragile stance—and there you sit
in a low lawn chair, reading, turning words
over. Then you look up. A smile.
A chat, a hug, and as I walk away,
I look back. There you sit, slight as the tree:
your blue eye winks.

༄༅། །སྲིད་གསུམ་མི་བརྟན་སྟོན་ཀའི་སྤྲིན་དང་འདྲ། །
།འགྲོ་བའི་སྐྱེ་འཆི་གར་ལ་ལྟ་དང་མཚུངས། །
།འགྲོ་བའི་ཚེ་འགྲོ་ནམ་མཁའི་གློག་འདྲ་སྟེ། །
།རི་གཟར་འབབ་ཆུ་ལྟ་བུར་མྱུར་མགྱོགས་འགྲོ། །

Like autumn clouds, the three existences are transient.
Like in a dance, see the birth and death of living beings.
Like a flash of lightning, the lifetime of a being rushes
like a cascading waterfall down a mountain.
　　—Lalitavistara Sutra, Chapter 33, 181b

The Waterfall

Water, borne by wind,
shatters rocks. Sand grains wash out and in,
the broken hourglass lifts and settles
a continual treadmill
round and round
settling grains into fissures
out in, out in.

Though swirled, the sand remains unagitated, unlike
our minds, unsettled by the inevitable ebb and flow.
Last fall, leaves fell unnoticed. Decay festered on the surface,
but a skirt from dancing covered the missteps.
Submerged in water, blisters bandaged, our shouts
were unheard by the crash of the waterfall,
a freefall into an abyss
where gradually a trickle of water
drained into a still pool.
A mist refreshes my face.
Looking in, I see my reflection
shifting in ripples.

Reading Before the Lines

Breaths from sorrow—ignite—a flame. Your smile:
Above, when truth ascends, present future takes heed.
Reason wends its way through this slick of lies.
Around you, we may grieve, yet you—are there.
Constellation clusters spell your name in prayer:
Kindness, knowledge, grace, and hope remain indestructible.

O, we have known goodness, though some refuse.
Before, we knew no hatred could destroy
A man whose heart was love, so trust and faith remain.
Many desire these traits, not ever having them.
As deception wearies, the most rugged crags smooth.

Fare Well

Breathing winter night,
Lambs turn their heads to heaven.
Ever brighter stars
Send comet tails streaking smiles
Spinning to Earth a message:

Inside a pocket
No smaller than galaxies
Grow happinesses

Searching to wish you good tidings.

About the Author

Annie Bien is a writer and a translator of Tibetan Buddhist texts into English. She received her first writing grant with a seed commission from the Soho Theatre Company in London. She has published poetry and prose in literary journals, been a Pushcart nominee, won third place in the Biscuit Poetry competition, and been a finalist in the Strokestown Poetry Competition. Her poetry collection, *Plateau Migration*, was published by Alabaster Leaves Press in 2012. Her translation work is supported by 84000, Translating the Words of the Buddha. She also teaches Pilates, and lives in Brooklyn.

www.ingramcontent.com/pod-product-compliance
Lightning Source LLC
LaVergne TN
LVHW021626080426
835510LV00019B/2778